MW01202179

THE GREAT GATSBY

by
F. Scott Fitzgerald

Teacher Guide

Written by
Maureen Kirchhoefer, M.A.
and Mary Lovejoy Dennis

Note

The softcover edition published by Collier Books/Macmillan Publishing Company, © 1925 by Charles Scribner's Sons was used to prepare this guide. The page references may differ in other editions.

Please note: Please assess the appropriateness of this book for the age level and maturity of your students prior to reading and discussing it with your class.

ISBN 1-56137-316-8

Copyright infringement is a violation of Federal Law.

© 2000, 2004 by Novel Units, Inc., Bulverde, Texas. All rights reserved. No part of this publication may be reproduced, translated, stored in a retrieval system, or transmitted in any way or by any means (electronic, mechanical, photocopying, recording, or otherwise) without prior written permission from Novel Units, Inc.

Photocopying of student worksheets by a classroom teacher at a non-profit school who has purchased this publication for his/her own class is permissible. Reproduction of any part of this publication for an entire school or for a school system, by for-profit institutions and tutoring centers, or for commercial sale is strictly prohibited.

Novel Units is a registered trademark of Novel Units, Inc.

Printed in the United States of America.

To order, contact your local school supply store, or—

Novel Units, Inc.
P.O. Box 433
Bulverde, TX 78163-0433

Web site: www.educyberstor.com

Table of Contents

About F. Scott Fitzgerald

F. Scott Fitzgerald is considered to be one of the primary spokesmen of the era he named the "Jazz Age"—the period beginning with the end of World War I in 1918 and ending with the stock market crash in 1929. He has become a kind of cult hero due to his tragic life, his early death, and his still-relevant exposés of the loss of the American Dream to the decadent materialism that proliferated with particular virulence during Fitzgerald's lifetime.

A native of St. Paul, Minnesota, Fitzgerald grew up in a family that was only moderately well-off. His boyhood and adolescence were spent acquiring the proper manners and learning the strict social code of upper-class Midwestern urban life. His family's Irish Catholicism and the strict Protestant moral standards of the Bible Belt provided him with unquestionable guidelines for irreproachable, albeit pretentious, behavior.

He was sent to prep school in New Jersey and then enrolled at Princeton University. He served in the U.S. Army from 1917-1919, but saw no overseas service.

In 1920, Fitzgerald married Zelda Sayre and began his career as a published writer with *This Side of Paradise,* an immediate best-seller.

The remaining twenty years of Fitzgerald's life were a kind of roller-coaster ride. When he and Zelda were expecting their daughter, they moved back to St. Paul because of a feeling that the East was an unsuitable place for an innocent child to live. Before long, they had relocated, to Long Island, then began to divide their time between the French Riviera, Paris, New York, and Rome. Fitzgerald also worked as a Hollywood scriptwriter, and he spent lots of time on the west coast.

Zelda, who had always been rather unstable, had a nervous breakdown in 1930, and by 1934 she was declared insane and had to be institutionalized. In the following year, the period known as Fitzgerald's "crack up" began. His long-standing problems with alcohol intensified. He was living in the "fast lane" in Hollywood, and his relationship with Sheilah Graham was a topic for gossip on a national scale. Fitzgerald died of a heart attack in 1940 at the age of only 44.

The Great Gatsby is considered to be his finest work and, in fact, one of the classic masterpieces of American literature. Not merely a chronicle of American society in the twenties, it succeeded in being what Fitzgerald envisioned when the novel was still in its planning stages: "extraordinary and beautiful and simple and intricately patterned."

 All rights reserved

It is a novel that almost all students can enjoy for its romantic-tragic story. They will also find it easy to relate the novel's themes to their own lives, values, dreams, and to their society.

The 1974 film version, starring Robert Redford and Mia Farrow, is eminently deserving of the awards it received and is a highly-recommended addition to the study of the novel.

Historical Background of the Jazz Age

The World War I Armistice was signed in November of 1918, and the following year saw the ratification of the Prohibition Amendment. This highly controversial legislation against alcohol was considered a "moral triumph" of the rural middle class over less morally-bound city sophisticates.

Prohibiting alcohol made little difference to the rich, however, as they could obtain it easily for a price. The illegal liquor traffic enriched gangsters, who controlled both the speakeasies and private distribution systems. Graft, extortion, protection rackets, and prostitution accompanied bootlegging and became the basis for a network of organized crime.

In 1920, the Women's Suffrage Amendment was ratified, and during the same year a national census revealed that the U.S. population was, for the first time, more urban than rural. Warren G. Harding was elected president on the platform "nationalism and normalcy." During his administration, there was minimal interference with business by the government, and fortunes were made. Harding is today remembered for the scandals that occurred during his tenure, for instance, the Teapot Dome oil scandal. Harding died in 1923 and was succeeded by Calvin Coolidge. Government had never been more subordinate to business.

From 1923-1929, industrial output nearly doubled. Americans were hungry for the acquisition of material goods, and mechanization put more and more products within the reach of more and more people. The middle class dollar—and the necessity of manipulating it—grew increasingly important to manufacturers. During these six years, a mere 5% of the population received one-third of the country's income, while 87% of families lived on less than $2500 a year. The escapades of wealthy people such as corporate leaders and movie stars became the chief entertainment of the middle class: although they were seen as pleasure-seekers living sinful lives, the public was enthralled.

The Jazz Age ended with the stock market crash in 1929. Fortunes that were made quickly and often illegally and at the expense of others, were lost. The country was thrown into the Great Depression.

The Great Gatsby

Plot Summary

The Great Gatsby is narrated by Nick Carraway, who describes himself as a "person inclined to reserve judgements." Recently discharged from the army, Nick leaves his well-to-do Midwestern home in the summer of 1922. He is headed for New York, where he plans to learn the bond business.

He rents a modest home on West Egg, Long Island—next to the palatial mansion of Jay Gatsby, a mysterious figure who hosts endless and extravagant parties for anyone and everyone who happens in, but who seems to be lonely and rather uninvolved with his guests.

Nick visits his second cousin, Daisy Buchanan, in East Egg (where the people with "old money" live). Daisy is beautiful and charming, but exudes an air of bored sophistication. Her friend and house guest Jordan Baker, a professional golfer, is haughty and discontented. When the phone rings and both Daisy and Tom Buchanan disappear into the other room, Jordan coolly informs Nick that the brutish Tom has "a woman in New York."

One afternoon, Nick and Tom are on the train to the city, and Tom insists they disembark near a desolate ash-dumping ground so that Nick can meet Tom's "girl," Myrtle Wilson. Myrtle's husband, George, runs a not-too-prosperous garage near the ash-heap and appears to know nothing about the affair. Myrtle meets them later in New York, and they spend the evening at Tom's city apartment, inviting Myrtle's sister and some neighbors in. In the drunken hours that follow, Nick is thoroughly sickened by the middle-class people's attempts to act sophisticated, which they do primarily by displaying their bigotry. The evening ends when Tom and Myrtle fight, and Tom hits her, breaking her nose.

Nick is formally invited to a party at Gatsby's, and he soon realizes the guests know little about their host, although there is a good deal of speculation about how Gatsby's fortune was made and why he is so distant. Nick finally meets Gatsby and agrees to go hydroplaning with him the next day. It seems Gatsby has taken a liking to Nick, though the reason is not immediately apparent.

As the summer wears on, the pointless parties next door continue. Nick remembers a golf scandal involving Jordan Baker, and begins to see that she is a very dishonest person. He sees her often nonetheless, but has little feeling or admiration for her.

In late July, Nick has lunch with Gatsby and is regaled with a dazzling but partially fictitious autobiography. He also meets Mr. Wolfsheim, a definitely shady business associate of Gatsby's, who asks Nick if he is "looking for a business gonnegtion." Nick is later appalled to learn that Wolfsheim fixed the World Series in 1919, and even more horrified that Gatsby takes it so lightly.

Later that afternoon, at a tea arranged by Gatsby, Jordan Baker reveals the real reason for Gatsby befriending him. It seems that Daisy and Gatsby were lovers five years previously when Gatsby was stationed near Daisy's home in Louisville. Jordan also describes the day before Daisy's wedding to Tom Buchanan—how she clutched a letter tightly in her hand and mumbled drunkenly that she had changed her mind about getting married. The wedding proceeded, although Tom was almost immediately caught philandering. Daisy soon gave birth to their daughter, and the Buchanans traveled to Europe, lived in Chicago for a while, and finally settled "for good" in East Egg.

Jordan further explains that Gatsby has spent all this time keeping track of Daisy, and has bought the house in West Egg just to be near her. Gatsby wants Nick to invite Daisy for tea—alone—so that he can "drop in" and see her. Nick agrees, the tea goes as planned, and Gatsby comes alive as his dream seems to be coming true.

At this point in the narrative, we read the "true" story of Jay Gatsby—actually James Gatz of North Dakota, the son of a poor farmer who became a sort of Man Friday for the millionaire Dan Cody, from whom he inherited $25,000 and the knowledge he needed to quickly make his own fortune.

One extremely hot August day, Gatsby and Nick are invited to the Buchanans. They all decide to drive to town, Gatsby and Daisy in Tom's coupe and the others in Gatsby's large yellow Rolls Royce, with Tom at the wheel. When Tom stops at Wilson's Garage for gas, he's informed by George that he's taking Myrtle West whether she likes it or not. Myrtle is nowhere in sight, but she sees Tom from the upstairs window and makes the assumption that Jordan is his wife.

Daisy, Gatsby, Tom, Nick, and Jordan rent a suite at the Plaza Hotel and begin drinking. There is a confrontation between Tom and Gatsby. Gatsby insists Daisy has loved only him since the day they met, and at first Daisy corroborates this. But when Tom begins to reveal the truth about Gatsby—his poor beginnings, his illegal activities—Daisy is repulsed. She finally says weakly that she loves them both, which totally crushes Gatsby. To show his lack of concern over the alliance, Tom insists that Daisy and Gatsby drive home together, this time in Gatsby's car.

© Novel Units, Inc.

All rights reserved

When they follow a little later, Nick, Tom, and Jordan see the aftermath of an accident in front of Wilson's garage. Myrtle Wilson has been killed by a hit-and-run driver—a speeding yellow car.

When Nick arrives at the Buchanans, he is so sick of them and their selfish hypocrisy that he doesn't even go into the house. As he waits for a taxi outside, he discovers that Gatsby is there, watching the house to "make sure Daisy is all right." Nick correctly guesses that Daisy was driving the car. Gatsby is heroically planning to claim that he was the driver. Nick goes closer to the house and sees through the window that Tom and Daisy are meeting conspiratorially in the kitchen, deciding what to do.

Wilson, insane with grief, traces the car to Gatsby and shoots him in his swimming pool, then commits suicide. Suddenly, Nick seems to be the only friend Gatsby has. Tom and Daisy have left town. Meyer Wolfsheim "cannot get mixed up in this thing." Except for one strange fellow who had been impressed by Gatsby's library, none of the party-goers are able to attend Gatsby's funeral.

The only family member who attends is Gatsby's pathetic father, who tells Nick about the Jimmy Gatz who had such great aspirations for the future and who was so filled with the idealistic hope that he, too, could be part of the American Dream. His father does not see that the dream is destroyed. He is simply proud of the wealth his son has attained.

Nick himself is unable to remain in the "haunted" East. He says goodbye to Jordan Baker with mixed feelings, and takes one last look at the Gatsby mansion. Nick realizes that Gatsby really thought he could grab the dream from his past, not realizing it was already far behind him, just as the American Dream died with people like Davy Crockett and Dan Cody.

As Nick looks ahead into his own life, he thinks about the hopes for the future in a new land that the Dutch must have had when they landed on Long Island, and he realizes that we all reach out hopefully to a future that very quickly becomes the past.

Prereading Activities

1. *The Great Gatsby* was published in 1925, in the midst of the roaring twenties. Providing students with background information on this time period (page 4) will improve their understanding of the novel and what society was like when it was written. Note that Fitzgerald is credited with having named this time period the Jazz Age.

2. Have the students complete the Anticipation Guide found in the *Novel Units Student Packet* for *The Great Gatsby.*

3. Provide brief information on F. Scott Fitzgerald's life (page 3).

4. As a whole class, or in small groups, have students brainstorm and list phrases and thoughts related to the following words:

   - great
   - romantic
   - idealistic
   - sophisticated
   - wealthy
   - realistic

   Ask which words they think belong together, i.e., are wealthy people always sophisticated? Are romantics realistic? Do you have to be wealthy to be great? They should justify their answers by giving examples or well-reasoned arguments.

5. Discuss New York City with the students. What makes it special as far as the arts are concerned? Why would it be advantageous for an aspiring actor or actress, artist, musician, or writer to live in or near New York? On a map, locate Long Island.

6. Discuss the concept of the American Dream with the students. To get them started, you might ask them to think of the reasons why people emigrate to America even today.

© Novel Units, Inc.

All rights reserved

Vocabulary • Discussion Questions
Writing Ideas • Activities

Chapter One

Vocabulary:

privy 1	communicative 1	plagiaristic 1	levity 1
abortive 2	elations 2	epigram 4	superficial 5
sinister 5	reproach 6	turbulence 6	supercilious 7
languidly 12	extemporizing 15	peremptorily 20	intimation 21

Discussion Questions:

1. What advice did the narrator's father give him?
   When he feels like criticizing anyone, he should remember that all the people in this world haven't had his advantages.
2. What have been the results of the narrator's habit of reserving judgement?
   He has been the often-unwilling recipient of the "intimate revelations" of many men.
3. What is the narrator especially careful not to forget?
   his father's suggestion that "a sense of the fundamental decencies is parcelled out unequally at birth"
   Do you agree with Nick's father? What are "fundamental decencies"?
4. What use of foreshadowing is utilized by Fitzgerald?
   The narrator's comment about his "unaffected scorn" for Gatsby is our first glimpse into the name behind the novel.
5. Explain what West Egg and East Egg are.
   The "eggs" are two unusual formations of land on Long Island, which extends due east of New York City. The two egg-shaped formations are separated by a bay. East Egg is more fashionable. Nick rents a small house on West Egg.
6. Who lives next to the narrator? Describe his house.
   Nick's next-door neighbor is Gatsby, and his mansion resembles the Hôtel de Ville in Normandy. It has a tower on one side, ivy climbing its walls, a marble swimming pool, and forty acres of lawn and garden.
7. Who are the Tom Buchanans and where do they live?
   The Buchanans live in one of the "white palaces" of East Egg. Daisy Buchanan is Nick's second cousin, once removed. Her husband, Tom, and Nick knew one another at Yale, where Tom was a football hero.

8. Tom's physical description is important later in the novel. How does the narrator describe him?
   a sturdy straw-haired man of thirty; had been one of the most powerful ends that ever played football at New Haven; arrogant eyes and a powerful body—a "cruel" body; gruff and aggressive

9. Describe Daisy. From the description, what actress, singer, or other well-known figure do you think might be like Daisy?
   Daisy has a "low, thrilling voice," a sad and lovely face, bright eyes, and a bright, passionate mouth. Her most alluring asset is her voice.

10. Describe Jordan Baker, and why she is at the Buchanans.
    Jordan, a girlhood friend of Daisy's, is their house guest. She is tall and slender, has gray eyes and a wan, charming, discontented face. She speaks contemptuously of West Egg because people who live there do not have the "old money" of the East Egg residents.

11. How do we get the distinct impression that Tom is a racist? What is his explanation for "civilization going to pieces"?
    Tom calls whites the "dominant race" and asserts that they must keep control or people of color will destroy society.

12. What attitude do Daisy and Jordan have?
    bored sophistication, cynicism

13. According to Jordan Baker, who phoned Tom during dinner?
    his girlfriend in New York

14. To what "secret society" do the Buchanans seem to belong?
    They seem to enjoy playing with other people's emotions as if life were nothing more than an amusing game.

15. How is Jordan shown as "immoral" and Daisy as innocent?
    Nick seems to remember a rather unpleasant story about Jordan. Daisy, even while playing word games, seems childlike.

16. What is the significance of the green light at the end of Chapter 1?
    Nick sees Gatsby outdoors late at night, reaching his arms out toward the green light. He seems mesmerized by it.

Question for Writing: Reread Daisy's comment right after her daughter was born. Do you agree with Daisy? Why or why not?

Activity: Distribute the Gatsby Discovery Sheet on the following page and have the students complete it as they read the novel. (Gatsby is a very mysterious figure at the beginning, and information about him is gradually revealed.)

Discovering Gatsby

After reading each chapter, note below the additional information you learn about Gatsby. Also jot down questions you have about him that you would like to see answered in successive chapters, and then watch for the answers as you read. Chapter 1 has been started for you.

Chapter	New Information Learned About Gatsby	Questions I Have About Gatsby
1	• lives in a mansion next to Nick • is fascinated by a green light on a dock across the bay	Why the light? Why did Daisy seem interested in him?

Chapter Two

Vocabulary:

grotesque 23	transcendent 23	contiguous 24	pastoral 28
ectoplasm 30	proprietary 30	hauteur 31	strident 36

Discussion Questions:

1. Describe the valley of ashes. What does it symbolize?
   It is a desolate area where empty people labor, watched over by the giant billboard eyes of Dr. T.J. Eckleburg. It symbolizes the "wasteland mentality" of the materialistic middle class and the spiritual emptiness of society as a whole. It is redolent of scenes from Dante's Inferno, *and is appropriately "watched over" by the huge, godlike eyes on the billboard.*

2. Does Tom try to keep his affair with Myrtle a secret?
   No. Everyone knows about it, and he often takes her to restaurants where he is likely to see friends. It is understood that his affair is nothing but an amusement.

3. Nick goes with Tom to visit Myrtle. Describe her and her husband, and what happens during the course of the evening.
   Myrtle, in her mid-thirties, is fairly stout but carries her surplus flesh "sensuously." She is full of vitality and yearns to escape her circumstances and acquire all the trappings of the wealthy. George, who runs an unprofitable garage near the valley of ashes, is "spiritless and anemic." Myrtle treats him badly. Nick and Tom stop at the garage, and Tom arranges for Myrtle to meet him in the city. At Tom's city apartment, they have an impromptu party with Myrtle's sister and some neighbors. Nick is repulsed by the lower-class people's attempts to emulate the wealthy. The evening ends with everyone getting drunk and Tom breaking Myrtle's nose for insisting on repeating Daisy's name over and over.

4. Explain the significance of the puppy episode.
   Myrtle's wish for the little dog is immediately fulfilled by Tom, but neither considers how she will be able to care for the puppy properly. He is just another possession. Ironically, the only person who seems to show any concern for the dog is the elevator boy, who brings milk and dog biscuits. Myrtle later refers to the boy as "shiftless."

5. What gossip about Gatsby does Nick learn at the party?
   Gatsby is supposedly the "nephew or cousin" of Kaiser Wilhelm.

6. What shows Myrtle's lack of sophistication?
   She uses poor grammar and speaks coarsely to her husband. She has lived with George over the garage for 11 years and Tom is her "first sweetie."

All rights reserved

Question for Writing: Why did Tom get so angry at Myrtle for mentioning Daisy's name? From his reaction, how do you think he feels about Daisy? About Myrtle?

Activity: Overindulgence in alcohol is a problem of many of the characters in *The Great Gatsby.* Have the students work in small groups to discuss characteristic behavior of people who have had too much to drink. They might make a list of appropriate adjectives, or use an attribute web like the one on page 23 as a framework for their discussion.

Chapter Three

Vocabulary:

cataracts 39	omnibus 39	fortnight 39	ravages 39
innuendo 40	prodigality 40	contemptuous 42	homogeneity 44
spectroscopic 45	impetuously 45	provocation 47	corpulent 49
provincial 49	echolalia 50	vinous 51	

Discussion Questions:

1. Gatsby's parties are juxtaposed to Tom's by Fitzgerald. How do they compare?
   Gatsby's parties are on a much grander scale, however the end results are not much different: everyone gets drunk and acts foolishly.
2. What does Nick mean when he says he is one of the few who were invited?
   Many people merely crash the parties given by Gatsby. He doesn't even know most of his guests.
3. What are some rumors about Gatsby heard at this party?
   He doesn't want any trouble with anybody. Someone says he once killed a man. Someone else says he was a German spy during the war.
4. What is Nick's comment about the gossip? What did he mean?
   "It was testimony to the romantic speculation he inspired that there were whispers about him from those who had found little that it was necessary to whisper about in this world" (page 44). Nick meant that the people at the party were rather wild and daring in their casual acceptance of all kinds of behavior, so their being in awe of Gatsby was remarkable.

© Novel Units, Inc.

All rights reserved

5. Who is "owl eyes" and what surprises him? Explain what he meant by Gatsby not cutting the pages.

   "Owl eyes" is a young man with large glasses who is impressed to discover that the books in Gatsby's library are real, not just cardboard covers for appearance. This tells us two things: that artifice is extremely common among the wealthy, and that Gatsby is not a "fake." Gatsby hadn't actually read the books, however, or the pages would have been cut apart at the edges.

6. What does Nick find most striking about Gatsby?

   that his smile has a quality of "eternal reassurance"

7. What about Gatsby is suspicious to Nick?

   that he seemed to drift out of nowhere to buy a palace on Long Island

8. What is ironic about Jordan's comment about large parties?

   She says they are more intimate than small parties, and it seems that it should be just the other way around.

9. What term of familiarity does Gatsby use when addressing Nick?

   "old sport"

10. What does Nick discover about Jordan later that summer?

    She is terribly dishonest. She lies about leaving a borrowed car out in the rain with the top down. Nick then recalls a past golf scandal in which she moved her ball to a better spot.

Question for Writing: Jordan Baker is dishonest, while Nick prides himself on his honesty. She is unconcerned about her bad driving because others will get out of her way. How might the two (bad driving and dishonesty) be connected, and why does Jordan feel comfortable with Nick?

Activity: As a whole-class activity, plan on the board a "dream party" of today that would approach the magnificence of Gatsby's.

Chapter Four

Vocabulary:

punctilious 64	disconcerting 65	retribution 65
somnambulatory 70	denizen 74	

Discussion Questions:

1. Nick keeps a list of the party guests on a train schedule dated July 5, 1922. Why did Fitzgerald include this section?
   This is Fitzgerald's social comment on East versus West. Names like Leeches, Catlips, Smirks, and Hammerheads are very suggestive of the character of the kinds of people who attended the parties. The people are snobbish, greedy users. The date on the timetable is important because it is the day after America's birthday—and this is what has happened to the American Dream of prosperity and equality. The timetable also helps the reader place the novel in 1922. Since Prohibition was in effect, we know the alcohol at the party is all illegal.

2. During a car trip, Gatsby tells his life story to Nick. Why doesn't Nick believe him? What proof does Gatsby offer?
   Gatsby seems to hurry over his explanation of his life, and says he's from San Francisco but calls it the Midwest. He does show Nick a medal of honor and a picture of himself at Oxford. Gatsby is trying to establish his credibility before he requests a favor of Nick.

3. What other travelers are seen just after Nick and Gatsby cross the Queensboro Bridge? Why are they important?
   A funeral procession passes just as Nick is thinking of the city's bright promise, pointing out that everyone's future ends with death, and possibly also alluding to the death of the American Dream. Nick is just thinking of people's awed reaction to Gatsby's splendid car when three Negroes being driven by a white chauffeur in a limousine pass by—a reminder that there are many kinds of "nouveau riche" people.

4. What is extremely unusual about Mr. Wolfsheim?
   The reader gets the immediate impression that he is a gangster or bootlegger. One of his friends was shot in his presence. His cuff links are made out of human molars. He asks Nick if he's looking for a "gonnegtion."

5. Note Wolfsheim's comment about Gatsby, "He would never so much as look at a friend's wife" (page 73). Why is it ironic?
   Gatsby is already trying to arrange to meet Daisy at Nick's.

6. What crime does Gatsby say Wolfsheim committed? What is Nick's reaction?
   Gatsby says that Wolfsheim fixed the 1919 World Series. Nick is flabbergasted.

7. Gatsby's unexpected departure from the restaurant upon meeting Tom is a transition for what Jordan is about to tell Nick in the next section of the chapter. What startling news does Nick discover about Daisy and Gatsby?
   They had been lovers in October, 1917, but Daisy's parents stopped her from going to New York to see him off to war. She married Tom despite the fact that she was still in love with Gatsby, who quickly used any and all means to acquire the wealth he knew he would need in order to claim Daisy as his own. He purposely bought the house across the bay to be close to her.

All rights reserved

8. What did Daisy do the day before her wedding to Tom?
   She got drunk and said she'd changed her mind. She was clutching a letter—presumably from Gatsby.
9. What was Tom doing shortly after the wedding?
   cheating on Daisy
10. What favor is asked of Nick on Gatsby's behalf?
    Gatsby wants Nick to invite Daisy to tea at his house, alone, so that he can see her again.

Question for Writing: Put yourself in Nick's place. A friend wants you to arrange a meeting with someone another friend is dating. What would you do? Why do you think Nick agreed?

Activity: Have several students find out more about the 1919 World Series. Discuss how fixing the series was a particular slap in the face of American ideals.

Chapter Five

Vocabulary:

harrowed 86	defunct 87	distraught 87	demoniac 88
vestige 90	postern 91		

Discussion Questions:

1. What does Gatsby propose that offends Nick?
   Gatsby offers to return the favor of making arrangements with Daisy by offering Nick a rather lucrative business deal. Nick refuses. He doesn't want to be "bought."
2. Describe Daisy and Gatsby's meeting.
   Have students discuss their observations and offer examples from their own experiences of unusual interpersonal encounters that made them feel either uncomfortable or especially happy (i.e., the first time they spoke with the person who is now their best friend, steady date, etc.).
3. How does the meeting with Daisy affect Gatsby?
   He literally glows with a new well-being.
4. How does Nick catch Gatsby in a lie?
   Gatsby says he earned his money. Earlier he said he inherited it.

5. Discuss the three emotional states Gatsby moves through upon meeting Daisy again.
   Gatsby was at first embarrassed and felt awkward, then filled with joy, and finally consumed with wonder.

6. Why do you think Daisy cries when she sees all of Gatsby's beautiful shirts?
   She may be crying over the "lost years" the accumulation of shirts represents, or she may simply be so materialistic that the sight of the expensive clothing brings her to tears of joy.

7. Why is Klipspringer unable to refuse Gatsby's request that he play the piano?
   Klipspringer is a non-paying self-invited "boarder" at Gatsby's. He apparently felt either an obligation to grant his host's wish, or a fear that he might be asked to leave if he didn't.

8. Why is the song "Ain't We Got Fun?" both appropriate and ironic?
   The song is about the rich and the poor, as is the novel. More importantly, it shows that society as a whole during this time was most interested in "having fun." Even though this is a solemn and romantic occasion, one which Gatsby has imagined for five years, the tune played by Klipspringer is rather artificial and shallow.

9. This chapter is often seen as the beginning of Gatsby's downfall. Offer suggestions as to how this might be true.
   Gatsby cannot see that Daisy is not like his idealized dream of her. Nick notes that Gatsby seems to "run down" like an overwound clock. The "colossal significance" of the green light is now vanished; the realization of the dream has begun, and there is no going back to the safety of fantasy, where one is totally in control.

10. Discuss with the students the expression, "Money can't buy happiness."

Question for Writing: Prove or disprove by citing examples from your own experience: the dream of what "could be" is usually superior to the dream achieved in reality.

Activity: Obtain and play recordings of several songs that were popular in the 1920s. Have the students listen closely to the words and "imagine" a video to accompany one of the songs. They might want to update the song by picturing it being performed by a favorite singer or group. Have them write descriptions of their imaginary videos.

Chapter Six

Vocabulary:

laudable 98	insidious 98	meretricious 99	ineffable 99
turgid 100	substantiality 102	antecedents 102	ingratiate 102
septic 107	euphemisms 108	dilatory 110	

Discussion Questions:

1. This chapter completes the narrative of Gatsby's life. Why is Fitzgerald's use of flashback more effective than chronological order?
    It creates suspense for the reader. By this time, we really want to know more about Gatsby. The illusory nature of his dream regarding Daisy is even more poignant when we read the true story of his life and his ill-gotten fortune.

2. Discuss Gatsby's five years as Cody's associate. Include his creation of a new persona.
    See pages 98-102. Gatsby is often compared to the archetypal European in the New World, while Cody is seen as the American frontiersman who showed him the ropes of attaining the American Dream, and yet who drifted aimlessly and without purpose.

3. Who unexpectedly drops in at Gatsby's one Sunday? What do you imagine is the reason for the visit?
    Tom and the Sloanes come by on horseback. Possibly Tom has some idea about Daisy and Gatsby, and hopes to catch her with him.

4. What does Gatsby flaunt at Tom?
    the fact that he knows Daisy
    What hypocritical remark does Tom make in reply?
    "...women run around too much these days to suit me."

5. Compare the behaviors of Tom and Gatsby.
    Tom is rude to Gatsby, leaving without him after Mrs. Sloane invited him to come to dinner. Gatsby, on the other hand, is innocently hospitable, offering the visitors drinks and saying the "right" things.

6. Nick notes that the illusion of one's world breaks down when outsiders enter it. Explain.
    At the party at Gatsby's, Daisy seems displeased with everything except the "scarcely human" movie star and her director. Daisy, too, wants to merely act out a role in her relationship with Gatsby. She is all artifice. Gatsby knows she didn't like the party, but he doesn't grasp what is really wrong with his relationship with Daisy.

 All rights reserved

7. The illusion is falling apart. Gatsby knows Daisy did not have a good time. What advice does Nick offer? How does Gatsby react?
Nick says you can't repeat the past, and Gatsby insists that you can. He has planned for five years to do just that, and he is unable to let go of the dream of recapturing the magic he once felt with Daisy—even though he has aggrandized the memories and created an impossible-to-attain illusion.

Question for Writing: Describe your life five years ago. What was important to you then? What gave you special pleasure? Is it possible now to repeat the same experiences and feel the same way about them? Would you want to?

Activity: Have the students divide into pairs or groups and present short skits based on the scenes in this chapter: (1) the Sloanes and Tom drop in at Gatsby's; (2) the Buchanans attend a party at Gatsby's; (3) Nick and Gatsby talk after the party. Encourage the students to use voice inflections and gestures that capture the mood of the novel.

Chapter Seven

Vocabulary:

indiscreet 120	boisterously 121	contingency 122	inviolate 125
explicable 126	portentous 128	vicariously 131	presumptuous 136
expostulation 139			

Discussion Questions:

1. Explain the reference to Trimalchio on page 113.
Trimalchio was a comic character in Petronius' Satyricon, also a "nouveau riche," known for his hilarious parties and farcical antics. Gatsby had given the parties in hopes that Daisy would eventually attend one. Now there is no need to continue them.
2. Describe the weather and its relevance to the plot.
It is very hot, perhaps to build dramatic tension as the story "heats up."
3. Explain how Pammy's appearance affects Gatsby.
She is out of harmony with his dream. Seeing her, he must admit she is real.

4. The Buchanans' unlimited wealth has left their lives empty and boring. Because of this, what does Gatsby represent for Daisy?
   He is simply a diversion and an amusing way to relieve the boredom; possibly he also offers her a way to pay Tom back for his infidelity. Daisy is a little girl playing "let's pretend." She has never experienced real life hardships and has never had to grow up.

5. What is Tom's hypocritical reaction to Daisy's affair?
   He suddenly becomes a "prig," acting like the guardian of morality and the American family. The double standard is at work here.

6. Gatsby aptly describes Daisy's voice as "full of money." Explain.
   Daisy is the embodiment of what Gatsby has been longing for all his life, but he might have better said that her voice is full of OLD money—something he can never have no matter how much wealth he accumulates. Gatsby doesn't seem to realize that there is a difference between the vulgar new wealth and the staid old wealth.

7. On the trip to the city, Tom drives Gatsby's car. What is ironic about Tom's comment, "You can buy anything at a drug-store nowadays"?
   He is actually referring to being able to buy bootleg liquor, and he later makes reference to Gatsby's "drug-store business." It is also ironic that he has "bought" Myrtle at a garage.

8. What has George Wilson learned?
   He knows that Myrtle is having an affair with someone. He wants to take her away.

9. Why has George, throughout the novel, been trying to buy a car from Tom?
   He knows he can make a quick profit on the sale of the car and get the money he needs to get out of town.

10. Compare Tom and George in their knowledge that their wives are having affairs.
    George wants to take Myrtle and run away; Tom is trying to act as if it is no big deal, that he is too important to really have to worry about Daisy and Gatsby.

11. What does Myrtle observe, and to what conclusions does she jump?
    When she sees Jordan in the car with Tom, she assumes she is Daisy.

12. Discuss the confrontation between Tom and Gatsby in the hotel.
    Gatsby insists Daisy denounce her marriage and love for Tom. Tom attacks Gatsby's business dealings. Daisy is affected by Tom's revelations, and "revises" her original stand to say that she loves "both" men.

13. Explain Nick's comment, "So we drove on toward death through the cooling twilight."
    Myrtle Wilson was killed on the road by Gatsby's speeding car.

14. How does Nick change as a result of Myrtle's death?
    He is suddenly sickened by Jordan and the Buchanans. He blames Tom's involvement with Myrtle for her death, but sees how unconcerned Jordan is with the situation.

  All rights reserved

15. Who did Myrtle think was driving the car? Who was really driving?
Myrtle ran out to the car because she had seen Tom driving it before. Perhaps she wanted to tell him of George's plan to take her West, and was going to confront Daisy with the affair. Daisy was actually driving the car, and Gatsby was her passenger.

Question for Writing: Gatsby remained outdoors, looking up at the light in Daisy's room, waiting to make sure she was all right. Meanwhile, Nick looked through the kitchen window and saw Tom and Daisy meeting in an almost conspiratory way. How is this scene a microcosm of the larger situation?

Activity: Use the Attribute Web framework on pages 22 or 23. Divide the students into five groups. Each group should discuss one of the main characters: Gatsby, Daisy, Tom, Nick, Jordan. Each group member should complete a web for their group's character. Then re-group the students so that each new group is composed of one representative for each of the five characters. Have the new student groups share their webs.

Chapter Eight

Vocabulary:

| grail 149 | stratum 149 | corroborate 154 | interminable 155 |
| garrulous 156 | pneumatic 161 | fortuitously 162 | holocaust 163 |

Discussion Questions:

1. What foreshadows Gatsby's death?
Nick has nightmares and wakes just before dawn with a feeling he must warn Gatsby about something—"and morning would be too late."
2. Nick urges Gatsby to go away, but he refuses. Explain.
Gatsby was still clutching at one last hope that Daisy would choose to be with him after all.
3. Why does Fitzgerald include Gatsby's flashback about Daisy?
It unravels a bit more of the mystery about Gatsby, this time giving the reader the real story of his feelings for Daisy.
4. To what "grail" does Gatsby refer?
As legendary heroes sought the Holy Grail at all costs, Gatsby has made Daisy his grail.

All rights reserved

Attribute Web

The attribute web below will help you gather clues the author provides about a character in the novel. Fill in the blanks with words and phrases which tell how the character acts and looks, as well as what the character says and what others say about him or her.

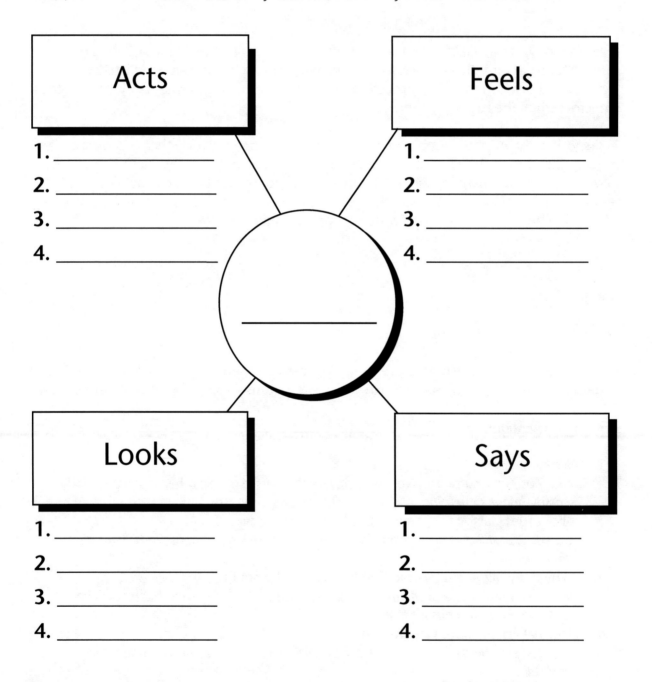

© Novel Units, Inc.

All rights reserved

Attribute Web

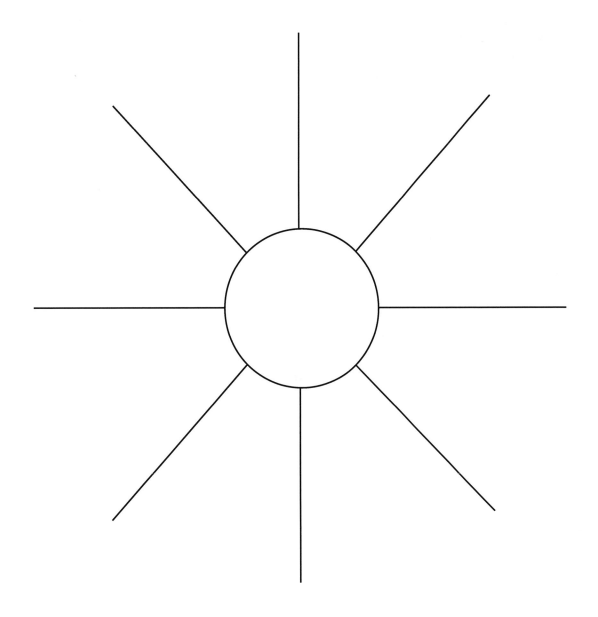

© Novel Units, Inc.

All rights reserved

5. What is the symbolic significance of autumn at the novel's end? Why is there a "sharp difference" in the weather?
   The falling leaves and the draining of the pool signal an end and parallel the end of the illusion and the end of Gatsby's life. On a larger scale, Gatsby's death symbolizes the death of the American Dream.

6. What does Nick mean when he says to Gatsby, "You're worth the whole damn bunch put together"? Is Nick being hypocritical?
   Although Nick disapproves of Gatsby's shady business dealings, and thinks he is a fool for believing he can recapture the past, he nonetheless admires his honest and steadfast devotion to a goal—Gatsby is still uncorrupted in that way, while all of the other characters are spiritually and morally bereft.

7. What does Nick realize about Jordan?
   Jordan is more concerned about herself than anything else. She is selfish and irresponsible, and he doesn't care if he ever sees her again.

8. George Wilson typifies the ordinary man. What else does Fitzgerald's portrayal of him suggest?
   Wilson lives in a world of delusion. He doesn't realize, even at the end, that Tom was Myrtle's lover all along. He mistakes Dr. Eckleburg's eyes for God's. With Tom's encouragement, he kills the wrong man and then himself, and is "reduced" to the label "deranged by grief." Wilson is seen as Tom Buchanan's scapegoat, just as the middle class in general is seen as the scapegoat of the rich.

Question for Writing: Reread the paragraph on page 162 beginning "No telephone message arrived…" How did Nick believe Gatsby was feeling during the minutes preceding his death? Do you agree with Nick's estimation?

Activity: Have students work in small groups to discuss the conversations that might have transpired between the following characters:
* Gatsby and Daisy on the way to New York
* Gatsby and Daisy on the way back to East Egg
* Tom and Daisy back home after the accident

Compare the various groups' versions.

All rights reserved

Chapter Nine

Vocabulary:

pasquinade 164   adventitious 164   deranged 164   solidarity 166
transitory 182   aesthetic 182

Discussion Questions:

1. The details of Gatsby's funeral are left to Nick. Why?
   No one else was interested in Gatsby in a personal way. They had used him for pleasure or for business profit, but had not really cared about him.
2. What seems to be of most concern to Klipspringer?
   his tennis shoes
3. Fitzgerald juxtaposes two views of Gatsby. What are they?
   Gatsby in his role as Wolfsheim's associate and Gatsby as the All-American son of Henry Gatz.
4. What does the call from Slagle tell the reader?
   It offers more evidence of Gatsby's criminal activities. Like the party-goers and Wolfsheim, Slagle has no personal interest in Gatsby. He assumes his death is the result of his business involvements.
5. Like Benjamin Franklin and Horatio Alger, Gatsby kept lists of his resolves. What do they represent?
   Gatsby's dreams of self-advancement began early. He believed in the American Dream.
6. Why does Nick tell Mr. Gatz he was a close friend of Gatsby's?
   Nick wanted to comfort the old man, who was obviously proud of his son and didn't realize that he hadn't attained the dream.
7. Why do you think Fitzgerald included the man with the owl-eyed glasses at the funeral?
   Student opinion, however owl-eyes seems to be used to help the reader "see." He alone noticed that Gatsby's books were real. He points out in the funeral scene that people used to come to Gatsby's by the hundreds, and he also sees that Gatsby was indeed a "poor son of a bitch."
8. How is *The Great Gatsby* a story of the West if it happened in the East?
   The characters are all what Nick calls "Westerners." (They are actually from what we now think of as the Midwest.) Nick feels they all possessed some common trait which made it impossible for them to adapt to Eastern life. The East is seen as an evil and grotesque place in the end, while Nick looks forward to the safe boredom of his Wisconsin home.

9. Discuss the carelessness of the Buchanans.
    They leave messes behind for others to straighten out. Tom is really responsible for the deaths of Myrtle, Gatsby, and Wilson, yet he leaves town and avoids any involvement. Daisy leaves the scene of the accident and is willing to have Gatsby take the blame. They leave town after Gatsby dies and let Nick take care of the funeral arrangements.

Question for Writing: Reread the last three paragraphs of the novel. Write in your own words what you believe Fitzgerald, through Nick, is saying.

Activities:

- Have the students complete the Review Sheets on pages 29-30, and then discuss the sheets with the whole class.

- Have the students complete story maps similar to the one on the following page.

- Complete a sociogram for Daisy or another character, using the framework below.

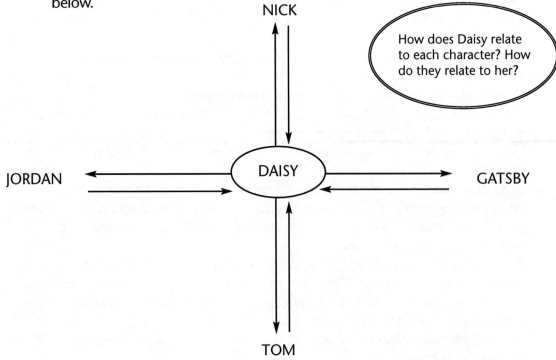

NICK

How does Daisy relate to each character? How do they relate to her?

JORDAN   DAISY   GATSBY

TOM

© Novel Units, Inc.   All rights reserved

Story Map

Characters_____

_____

Time and Place_____

_____

Problem_____

_____

_____

Goal_____

_____

_____

Beginning ——→ Development ——→ Outcome

_____

_____

_____

_____

Resolution_____

_____

_____

_____

_____

Setting

Problem

Goal

Episodes

Resolution

Film Review

TITLE OF FILM: _____

BASED ON THE NOVEL: _____

Movies based on novels are often different than the books on which they are based. Imagine you have been given a "sneak preview" of this film before it is released to the public. In exchange, the producers want your opinions on the following questions.

1. What are the main differences between the film and the novel?

    _____

    _____

    _____

    _____

    _____

2. Compare a character from the book with a character in the film. Was the character the way you pictured him/her? Is there another actor who would have been a better choice?

    _____

    _____

    _____

    _____

3. How did the movie help you to better understand the book? Please be specific.

    _____

    _____

    _____

© Novel Units, Inc.   All rights reserved

Critic's Assistant

Various critics have offered the following as possible themes of *The Great Gatsby*. For each theme statement, cite an example from the novel that the critic might offer to support his or her opinion.

1. The idealistic American Dream has been replaced by materialism and greed.

2. The West has its simple virtue; the East is corrupt and evil.

3. Wealth is power. Wealth and power corrupt.

4. Belief in romantic destiny has dire consequences.

Symbols and Motifs

Briefly describe the significance of each symbol or motif.

1. East Egg/West Egg

2. the green light

3. the valley of ashes

4. Dr. T. J. Eckleburg

5. Seasons (summer, fall)

6. the color white

7. Gatsby's parties

8. alcohol

© Novel Units, Inc.

All rights reserved

Bibliography

Bloom, Harold, Ed. *F. Scott Fitzgerald's The Great Gatsby. Modern Critical Interpretations Series.* Chelsea House Publishers, New York: 1986.

Donaldson, Scott. *Critical Essays on F. Scott Fitzgerald's The Great Gatsby.* G.K. Hall and Co., Boston: 1984.

Lehan, Richard. *The Great Gatsby: The Limits of Wonder.* Twayne's Masterwork Studies. G.K. Hall and Co., Boston: 1990.

Lockridge, Ernest, Ed. *Twentieth Century Interpretations of the Great Gatsby.* Prentice-Hall, Inc., Englewood Cliffs: 1968.

Mizener, Arthur, Ed., *F. Scott Fitzgerald: A Collection of Critical Essays.* Prentice-Hall, Inc., Englewood Cliffs: 1964.

Way, Brian. *F. Scott Fitzgerald and the Art of Social Fiction.* St. Martin's Press, New York: 1980.

Answer Key

Review Sheet #1: Theme

(1) Gatsby is the tragic, romantic hero who still believes in the American Dream. Part of his plan for self-advancement is an idyllic romantic alliance with Daisy, the only "nice" girl he has ever known. But love alone is not enough; he knows he must have tremendous wealth to obtain Daisy, and he lets her believe he is already wealthy. To quickly cover up for this falsity, he allies himself with the criminal element. Eventually, this revelation destroys any chance of a life with Daisy, who finds his "new money" vulgar.

(2) The "old money" residents of East Egg are bored, sophisticated, and morally corrupt. West Egg is less fashionable, and Nick and Gatsby, who live there, are more honest and idealistic. All of the characters are from the West, and do not adapt well to life in the East. When George Wilson finds out about Myrtle's affair, he plans to "go West" as soon as he gets the money. At the end of the novel, Nick returns to the safe boredom and dependable morality of Wisconsin.

(3) Tom Buchanan is the symbol of power and ruthlessness. He carries on his literal experience as a football player by figuratively destroying anything that stands in his way. It is because of his affair with Myrtle that she, Gatsby, and Wilson all die, yet Tom escapes unscathed.

(4) Gatsby's passionate belief in the dream of a life with Daisy was a grand illusion. He paid the highest price for believing they were destined to be together.

Review Sheet #2: Symbols and Motifs

East Egg/West Egg: old money/new money; the morally corrupt East vs. the still-virtuous West; Tom Buchanan's ruthless power vs. Gatsby's gentle faith in a hopeless dream

the green light: Gatsby's dream of a life with Daisy

valley of ashes: the "wasteland;" spiritual emptiness of the working class and their artless struggle for material wealth

Dr. T.J. Eckleburg: seen by Wilson as "the eyes of God"; spiritual and religious values corrupted

seasons: summer is the fruition of Gatsby's dream and the American Dream, the hope of all that will be; autumn is the end of the dream, the end of Gatsby's life, the end of American idealism

the color white: Daisy and Jordan's apparent innocence and morality, in reality an absence of either as white is the absence of color

Gatsby's parties: money can buy only the illusion of gaiety and friends; money can't buy love

alcohol: This illegal source of Gatsby's wealth is also what fuels his parties and causes problems throughout the book: Tom is drunk when he breaks Myrtle's nose; in the confrontation scene, everyone is drinking. It symbolizes moral decay and evil.

© Novel Units, Inc.

All rights reserved